The Global Pogrom

By Benjamin Kerstein

The following essays are reprinted by permission of The Tower magazine, which can be accessed at http://www.thetower.org/magazine/.

Cover photo by David Gott

Table of Contents

Everything that needs to be said has already been said. But since no one was listening, everything must be said again.

—Andre Gide

The Global Pogrom

There is a Global Pogrom under way.

This is a terrible truth. And people tend to ignore terrible truths. So it must be said again: There is a Global Pogrom under way.

And another terrible truth must be spoken: The Global Pogrom has been under way for more than a decade. It has taken lives. It has destroyed property. It has injured, brutalized, and terrified Jews and Jewish communities in many nations. And it is creating a silent exodus, a de facto expulsion, an ethnic cleansing in slow motion.

To say again, because it must be said again, this is something almost no one wants to admit. A truth that almost no one, including many Jews, wants to speak or hear. But over the past month, it has become a truth that is impossible to ignore.

Yet even in the face of this, many continue to deny it, or at least to minimize it. And many, one regrets, have chosen to blame it on the Jews themselves.

A mere seven decades after the Holocaust, after the world was supposed to have learned its lesson, this is not only monstrous. It is not only evil. It is also an existential threat to the civilized world. Because the Global Pogrom presents the world with a stark choice: The Global Pogrom or civilization. And a civilization, any civilization, that cannot or will not say no to barbarism, is no longer a civilization at all.

The moment when, at long last, the Global Pogrom became impossible to deny took place in France. This is not surprising, as France has been the epicenter of the phenomenon from the moment it began. But this time, the violence was so savage, its target so public, and the perpetrators so obvious, that no one but the most demented apologists could pretend it did not happen.

On July 13, 2014, as the war between Israel and Hamas intensified, an ostensibly pro-Palestinian demonstration in Paris quickly devolved into the pogrom that, perhaps, it was always meant to be. A mob of thugs descended upon the Synagogue de la Roquette, trapped the congregation inside, and tried to break in while brandishing deadly weapons.

One of those trapped was a woman who, perhaps for fear of reprisal, asked to be identified only as Aurélie A. Her testimony, translated in Tablet magazine, describes a horrific scene.

Initially mobbed outside the synagogue, she sees one of the "protesters" "shouting 'Death to the Yids!'" She quickly realizes "the magnitude of the situation… They've surrounded us… We hear cries everywhere… I see firearms fly… I even see a man with an axe." The outnumbered French police, either terrified or simply uninterested, barely get her safe inside.

But "here we can no longer get out… the pressure inside rises. There are elderly people who feel oppressed, there are women who start to cry, in some places the volume rises. Then the first wounded… EMTs…" She looks through a window and "I saw as in a prison what was happening outside. More cries! They are still there… There are now hundreds!" In an instant, it comes to her: "The synagogue is under siege! The demonstrators want in!" And there is no doubt what they will do if they get in: "We can expect the worst."

The attack continues, the minutes pass by. The police appear to be unable or unwilling to disperse the attackers. But the police are not the only ones there. Outside the synagogue are members of Jewish defense organizations: The SPCJ, the community's official anti-Semitism watchdog organization with their own security force; the Revisionist youth group Beitar; and the Ligue de Defense Juive (LDJ), the French wing of the Jewish Defense League. To the eternal shame of the French police, Aurélie notes that "Our protectors act with courage, far more so than law enforcement, and rightly so, because *there were fewer armed men than Jews securing the synagogue…*" [emphasis mine].

The attackers hit the synagogue again. This time "projectiles multiply" and "I foresee wounded." "Time drags," she writes, "The children can't take it anymore... I light a candle..."

At long last, the thugs are brought under control, and the congregants are escorted out by the Jewish defense organizations "in small groups, escorting each of the faithful."

In perhaps the darkest passage of this very dark tale, Aurélie, who like most French Jews is of Sephardi descent, calls her father, who grew up in Algeria. She asks him if he had ever seen anything like the assault on the synagogue. He says, "Yes... In Algeria, before leaving it all behind... But we were in Algeria, here we're in metropolitan France!"

"Yesterday," she notes upon reflection, "a part of my love for France left me." And she is right to feel that way. France fancies itself a civilized nation, yet what she witnessed is nothing that a civilized nation would allow.

Aurélie is hardly alone in her testimony. Journalist Alain Azria witnessed the incident, and **stated simply**, "The anti-Israel protesters had murder on their mind." In another testimony to the shameful conduct of the authorities, he said of the Jewish defense groups, "Thank God they were there."

Another eyewitness **described** how the crowd threw "stones and bricks at the building, 'like it was an intifada.'" A Jewish leader made the horrifying statement, "We could have had something like Kristallnacht." The attackers, he said, "had rocks, glass, axes, knives... they were armed and I made sure that no one would leave the synagogue, in order to protect the lives of our people."

We have seen the likes of this before. Many times. Far too many times. There is only one word for mob attacks on Jews; attempts to defile and destroy Jewish houses of worship; the rampaging, sadistic, drooling desire to wound and kill defenseless human beings because they are Jewish; and the indifference, incompetence, or collaboration of non-Jewish authorities: *Pogrom*.

If what happened at the Synagogue de la Roquette is not a pogrom, then nothing is.

And French Jews themselves seem to sense this. That something has changed. That the country they live in, and whose principles of liberty, equality, and fraternity they have embraced as their own, no longer believes in any of these principles. Joel Mergui, a leader of the French Jewish community, put it in stark terms: "In people's minds," he said, "there will be a before and after the Synagogue de la Roquette."

Perhaps most appallingly, the la Roquette pogrom was met with another equally ancient atrocity: Pogrom Denial. Far-Left groups supportive of the demonstration, including the American hate site Mondoweiss, made two claims that have always been made about pogroms: First, it didn't happen. Second, maybe it might have possibly happened, but it was the Jews' fault.

They claimed that the pogrom was, in fact, nothing more than a street fight, and was instigated by the LDJ, something blatantly contradicted by eyewitnesses in and outside the synagogue, including Azria, who **wrote** that the pogromists "splintered off the main protest and headed to the synagogue. The Jewish defenders saw this because they were monitoring the demonstration and followed to put up a defensive fight."

Every pogrom in history has had its defenders. Slaughters like Kishinev have been called mere peasant uprisings, justified assaults on the Jews who economically exploited others, or attempts to "fight back" against the Jews who supposedly run the world. There have been innumerable other excuses. And indeed, there are just as many this time around.

The French Jews themselves, thankfully, are having none of it. CRIF, the umbrella group for French Jewry, attacked

the misrepresentation of the incident by some media. These attacks are passed off as inter-communal clashes, when in reality, these are hateful, violent and unilateral anti-Semitic attacks by pro-Palestinian and Islamist movements.

Said the president of CRIF, "I am shocked when I hear journalists saying if the de la Roquette synagogue was attacked, it is because of the Jews. This is propaganda."

The la Roquette Pogrom was merely the worst in a series of atrocities. A *Haaretz* report notes that another Paris synagogue was firebombed the Friday before. In addition, a man pepper-sprayed a Jewish teenager on a Paris street, telling her "Dirty Jewess, *inshallah* you will die." The girl in question also would not allow herself to be identified by name. In a Paris suburb, "demonstrators" declared their desire to "slaughter the Jews."

  The Pogrom did not die with the successful defense of la Roquette. Following the attack, the French authorities banned further anti-Israel demonstrations. The pogromists, as is their wont, marched anyway. And, as is again their wont, they went on a rampage, storming through the Jewish neighborhood of Sarcelles, destroying, looting, defacing, and generally acting like what Mayor François Pupponi later called "a horde of savages."

  "We never saw such hatred and violence as we witnessed in Sarcelles," said the mayor. "This morning people are astonished and the Jewish community is frightened." *The Jerusalem Post* interviewed the chief rabbi, Laurent Berros:

> The day before, flyers appeared encouraging demonstrators "to come fight with the Jews" and many came armed with hatchets and cudgels. "I stayed at the synagogue with the youth and the police trying to protect the community… lots of Jewish stores were burnt; the pharmacy, bank, tramway…the town has been really devastated."

The Huffington Post collected reports similar sentiments from other residents.

"They were shouting: 'Death to Jews,' and 'Slit Jews' throats,'" David, a Jewish sound engineer told The Times. "It took us back to 1938."

"We called our town 'Little Jerusalem' because we felt at home here," Laetitia, a longtime Sarcelles resident, told France 24. "We were safe, there were never any problems. And I just wasn't expecting anything like this. We are very shocked, really very shocked."

The horrors have still not ended. At yet another illegal demonstration on July 26 in Paris, protesters gave both the Nazi salute and its now-popular pogromist variation: The so-called "Quenelle," popularized by a virulently racist comedian in order to skirt France's laws against racial incitement.

The Pogrom has also spread into the virtual world. One group of self-styled "revolutionaries" created a Facebook page displaying names, photos, and addresses of 32 Jews and called for them to be attacked. The Jewish newspaper *Algemeiner* reported that "A violent mob of more than a dozen men in France assaulted a Jew at his home in a Paris suburb after confirming that his photograph" was on the page. The victim was beaten with iron bars and saved solely by the coincidental appearance of a neighbor, which caused the assailants to flee.

Hate speech and incitement to violence against Jews are flying at light speed across the Internet. A recent article in the Times of Israel described the travails of those who moderate comments on major French websites. In regard to Israel and the Jews, 90-95 percent of comments have to be blocked due to violent and racist content. "We see racist or antisemitic messages," said one moderator, "very violent, that also take aim at politicians and the media, sometimes by giving journalists' contact details." Another chillingly noted, "Calls for murder are our daily life. It's sometimes hard psychologically for our moderators."

To their credit, since the la Roquette and Sarcelles pogroms, French politicians and officials have been outspoken in their condemnation of the attacks. Although, given the ongoing violence, one must wonder at the sincerity of their words. Nonetheless, they have finally begun to acknowledge that the Pogrom exists, and something must be done about it.

French Prime Minister Manuel Valls, for example, stated unequivocally, "To attack a synagogue and a kosher grocery store is quite simply anti-Semitism and racism." The French interior minister visited Sarcelles, and said, "When you threaten synagogues and when you burn a grocery because it is Jewish-owned then you are committing antisemitic acts." While asserting the legitimacy of demonstrating against Israel, he nonetheless acknowledged, "Nothing can justify such violence."

Although the French Socialist Party has been traditionally ambivalent toward Israel, its president went so far as to call the pogromists "rampaging hordes." And he acknowledged the essential truth that "Nobody participates or supports an attack on a Jewish business without being part of a movement that threatens above all to lead civilization into barbarity."

In addition, Foreign Minister Laurent Fabius, who is no particular friend of Israel, publicly stated that "Jews in France should not be afraid, but many of them are afraid." His government, he said, "will be extremely firm" in dealing with the problem.

But this is, as the saying goes, far too little and far, far too late.

This is because the la Roquette and Sarcelles pogroms are not isolated incidents. They are outbreaks in a pogrom that has been ongoing for 14 years. This ongoing series of racist atrocities has killed, impoverished, exiled, and terrified many, while the authorities, for the most part, did nothing.

It began in late 2000, when the Palestinian Arabs rejected peace and embarked on a terrorist war against Israel. Simultaneously, pro-Palestinian Muslims and non-Muslims rose up around the world to support the terror war, and their tactics quickly turned from non-violent protest to pogromist campaigns of violent intimidation and destruction.

This occurred all over Europe, but France quickly became its epicenter. This was perhaps inevitable, since France has both the largest Jewish and the largest Muslim populations in Europe. But the Jews number only 500,000. While no one is quite certain of the Muslim population, it certainly numbers well into the millions. Faced with both the electoral power of its Muslim minority and the threat of social unrest and violence from this often restive community, French authorities have found it convenient to react to pogroms by simply ignoring them. This has held true even in the face of some of the most appalling atrocities to take place in France in decades.

In the Facebook assault mentioned above, the attackers apparently told their victim that they would do "the same as Ilan Halimi" to him. There is a reason for that. For many French Jews, the kidnapping, torture, and slaughter of the young Ilan Halimi in 2006 was a breaking point. The point at which, however much the French authorities might deny the ongoing progrom, the Jews no longer could or would.

Taken captive by a largely Muslim gang who appropriately named themselves "The Barbarians," Halimi was held prisoner for weeks and brutally tortured. He was finally dumped on a roadside by the killers, "naked and bleeding from at least four stab wounds to his throat, his hands bound and adhesive tape covering his mouth and eyes. According to the initial autopsy report, burns, apparently from the acid, covered 60 percent of his body." As *The New York Times* reported, "His captors told his family that if they did not have" ransom money, "they should 'go and get it from your synagogue,' and later contacted a rabbi, telling him, 'We have a Jew.'"

Police later ascertained that "at least 20 people participated" in Halimi's "abduction and the subsequent, amateurish negotiations for ransom." None of them did anything to save Halimi's life. Worse still, Pogrom Denialists quickly jumped on the ransom demands, claiming that the atrocity was linked to money and not anti-Semitism. The authorities, finding this excuse convenient, followed suit.

But the gang had apparently stalked four other Jewish men beforehand, and "The police found Islamist literature and documents supporting a Palestinian aid group in the home of at least one of the people arrested." When the *Times* asked a young French-Arab man what he thought of the gang leader, the man responded, "If the police bring him back here, the guys in the neighborhood will liberate him."

It is debatable as to whether something could be objectively "worse" than what was done to Ilan Halimi. But if such a thing exists, it would be the Toulouse Massacre. In early 2012, a demented racist named Mohammed Merah went on a killing spree. After shooting several French soldiers, he descended on the Ozar HaTorah children's school, where he killed a rabbi and his two sons before chasing down an 8-year-old and shooting her in the head. Another child was seriously injured.

Following Merah's death at the hands of the French police, the Denialists went into overdrive, attempting to blame Merah's act on economic deprivation, parental negligence, social alienation, etc., etc. *Anything* except anti-Semitism. Perhaps Europe's most prominent Denialist was the celebrated intellectual Tariq Ramadan, who said, "[Merah's] political thought is that of a young man adrift, imbued neither with the values of Islam, or driven by racism and anti-Semitism."

But Merah's own words and those of his brother proved otherwise. Shortly before his death, Merah reportedly told police he had committed his atrocity to "avenge Palestinian children." And his brother, Abdelghani, presented the most damning evidence, stating that radical Islam and anti-Semitism, stemming from their parents, had made Mohammed kill. "My parents raised you in an atmosphere of racism and hate," he said. "My mother always said: 'We, the Arabs, we were born to hate Jews.' This speech, I heard it all throughout my childhood."

The Toulouse slaughter was echoed on July 28, 2014, when in a thoroughly heinous act, a pogromist hurled three firebombs at the city's Jewish community center. Once again, the attack originated in an anti-Israel demonstration.

Until the la Roquette and Sarcelles pogroms, the Halimi atrocity and the Toulouse massacre were merely the worst incidents of anti-Jewish violence in recent years. For the most part, however, this has been a pogrom in slow motion, an accumulation of thousands of smaller atrocities: Incidents of violence, intimidation, vandalism, indignity, and the cultivation of fear that have had their inevitable—and no doubt intended—effect.

As a BBC report indicated earlier this year, large numbers of French Jews are now "'afraid to be Jewish' in France" due to "a rise in anti-Jewish hate crimes in the country." The report might have been very tardy, but it is telling.

For 2013, it notes 423 antisemitic incidents. And one must assume that many more go unreported as a result of the intimidation that led the aforementioned witnesses to conceal their names. Even more startling is the news that "40 percent of all racist violence perpetrated in France targeted Jews." In the networks' typically understated style, the BBC noted, "antisemitic attacks in France are reported with some regularity."

The results, for an ostensibly civilized 21st century nation, are appalling: "French Jews often fear outwardly appearing Jewish. A European Union survey published recently suggested that 40 percent of Jews in France will avoid wearing clothing that identifies them as being Jewish." Looking at the three examples of antisemitic incidents provided, one quickly understands why.

> In March, a 59-year-old Jewish teacher was severely beaten by a group of young men who cursed him, broke his nose and drew a swastika on his chest with a marker.
> Earlier that month, a young Jewish woman was assaulted at a laundromat in a suburb of Lyon by a mother

and daughter of Arab descent who shouted, "Dirty Jew, go home to your country, Israel."

During a Paris rally in January, a day before Holocaust Memorial Day, at least 17,000 people marched in the streets while shouting "Jews, get out of France."

One of my own personal friends experienced such an incident. She was surrounded and threatened by a gang of Muslim youths on the Paris Métro, escaping only by the skin of her teeth. As she ran from the attackers, she begged a shop owner to hide her and call the police. He refused. He didn't want to get involved. Thankfully, she escaped unharmed despite his indifference. It was, she told me, the last straw. A few months later she moved to Israel. Permanently.

And all of this mayhem, it must be noted, happened long before a gang of thugs attacked a synagogue and sacked a "little Jerusalem." Throughout most of it, the French authorities acted like the shop owner who abandoned my friend to a gang of thugs. They said little and did less. As always, it was not just that evil men were willing to do evil, but that good men were too cowardly or too indifferent to lift a finger to stop them.

The growing desperation of France's beleaguered Jews seems to be illustrated more than anything else by their growing embrace of self-defense groups like the LDJ. One older member of the community, Victor Sofer, seems to personify this shift. He told the Jewish Telegraphic Agency,

I used to tell my grandsons to focus on their studies and stay out of trouble, but now I sent them to join the LDJ and defend our synagogues against the scum. The Arabs own the streets now. We need make them lose the appetite for messing with us if we're to survive here. LDJ is our Iron Dome.

One community leader simply said, "The cops are here now, but it'll be just us and the Arabs tomorrow." Into this vacuum, it seems, is flowing the LDJ.

Were the Global Pogrom confined to France, it would not be necessary to call it "Global." It would simply be the "French Pogrom," which would be quite appalling enough. But France, due to its large Jewish and Muslim populations, as well as its longtime cultural propensity for mob violence, is simply the most prominent example. Over the last 14 years, it has become clear that this pogrom is Europe-wide.

Even before the latest explosion of anti-Jewish violence and hatred, Jews all over Europe were neither comfortable nor secure. A poll taken in 2013 showed that "Fear of rising anti-Semitism in Europe has prompted nearly a third of European Jews to consider emigration because they do not feel safe in their home country." To avoid distorting the data, the poll "focused on eight countries that account for more than 90 percent of Europe's Jewish population."

The reasons for these sentiments were amply on display over the past week, as a series of anti-Israel demonstrations across Europe promptly degenerated—or showed their true selves, depending on how you look at it—into open anti-Semitism.

In Antwerp, *Haaretz* reported, 500 people "protested" Israel's war in Gaza by listening to a speaker who used "a loudspeaker to chant a call in Arabic that means 'slaughter the Jews.'" Attendees "also called out 'Jews, remember Khaybar, the army of Muhammad is returning,' referencing a seventh-century slaughter against Jews in Saudi Arabia."

Such genocidal rhetoric was not confined to Belgium. It also appeared in, of all places, Germany. One would have thought that, in the post-Shoah age, Germany had lost the right to allow such things to occur. But this was not the case. A report from the Times of Israel states, "In Dortmund and Frankfurt anti-Israel protesters chanted, '*Hamas, Hamas, Juden ins gas*!' ('Hamas,

Hamas, Jews to the gas!'). On Friday, a 200-strong mob in Essen chimed in, '*Scheiss Juden!*' ('Jewish shit')."

In Berlin, once the seat of the Nazi regime, "An angry mob gathered" to spew language that would have enchanted the late Fuhrer. "Draped in Palestinian flags and shaking their fists in rage, they chanted in German, '*Jude, Jude feiges Schwein! Komm heraus und kämpf allein!*' ('Jew, Jew, cowardly swine, come out and fight on your own!')."

Most importantly, we should not make the common mistake of presuming that this pogromist rhetoric stems only from radical Muslim immigrants. A Global Pogrom does not discriminate. People of all races and creeds are happily invited. The mobs that gathered to spew genocidal hatred across Germany were "largely young, with both immigrants and native Germans.... Politically they span the spectrum, from German neo-Nazis to Marxist anti-Imperialists, from secular Palestinian nationalists to Islamic fundamentalists."

The role of Islam cannot be ignored, however. An imam was recently filmed in Berlin calling on God himself to commit genocide, asking him "not to spare a single one" of the Jews.

As in France, this constant incitement to violence and genocide has had its intended effect—the legitimization of pogromist behavior. Recently, according to the Times of Israel, a Jewish man "was attacked in Berlin for wearing a Star of David. A similar episode occurred in April when six youths surrounded an Israeli and his wife as they left their apartment building and physically assaulted the Israeli in the face."

In nearby Austria, the pogrom invaded one of Europe's last truly sacred places: The soccer field. During a friendly match between Lille and Maccabi Haifa, a group of thugs stormed the field and "tried to attack Yossi Benayoun, the national team captain, as well as other members of the squad. One player was spat on, while the coach entered the pitch to protect his players." Samuel Scheimann, another team member, "claimed at least one of the rioters was armed with a pocket knife."

In London, home to a large Muslim minority, a series of protests were, at least, fairly peaceful, but the rhetoric remained one of unrelenting incitement and defamation. One popular talking point is that Israel is guilty of genocide. Another is "Hitler, you were right." Such rhetoric is clearly intended to cause maximum pain and offense to Jews. A protest that uses such rhetoric is not a protest. It is an attack. At least one observer found the sight repulsive enough **to write**, "Thousands of anti-Semites have today succeeded in bringing central London to an almost total standstill."

This seems to be an understatement. The British Jewish community is now under siege as well. Death and bomb threats are flowing in by the dozen. Hate crimes are skyrocketing. A Jewish boy was the target of stone thrown by a Muslim woman. A rabbi was the target of a gang attack. Chants of "Heil Hitler" are defiling Jewish neighborhoods.

In a strange way, however one of the most disturbing stories to emerge from this Europe of the Global Pogrom is also one of the least violent. When Swedish pro-Israel activist Annika Hernroth-Rothstein, perhaps Sweden's most prominent pro-Israel activist, arrived to Israel a week ago to express her solidarity, she found that her suitcase had been vandalized, likely due to the horrendous crime of bearing a small Israeli flag.

"I opened my bag," she said in an online interview,

> and someone has poured soda on my things, the bag is obviously cut with some kind of sharp instrument, and the flag once stitched to it is now half-gone. Worst of all, to me, is that my siddur [the traditional Jewish prayer book] is wet and damaged. I have kept that from when I first started going to [synagogue], it is a fond memory of my journey back to observant life. When I found it I cried like a baby.

Perhaps this incident sticks in the mind for a simple reason: If this hatred is so low, so cowardly and petty, as to motivate such a violent attack on an inanimate object, what more would it be capable of inflicting on a human being? Unfortunately, we already know the answer.

In recent days, it has become increasingly clear that the Global Pogrom does not end at the borders of Europe. It is easy for the Jews of North America, long inured to societies that do not share Europe and the Middle East's long histories of anti-Semitism, to pretend that it will not or cannot happen to them. That the Pogrom will not or cannot reach them.

Recent days have proven this sadly false. The Pogrom has reached North America, like the first symptoms of a terminal disease. As in Europe, the Pogrom is based in ostensibly anti-Israel protests and demonstrations that traffic in racist and defamatory rhetoric, and ultimately erupt into mob violence.

The problem is already serious enough to force the Anti-Defamation League to issue a security warning to Jewish institutions across the United States. A spokesman told the Times of Israel,

> The warning is in response to the violence and anti-Semitic expressions that we have seen at some of these demonstrations. The tenor of some of these demonstrations has been extreme, with protesters chanting, "Death to Israel" and other hateful messages and slogans.

He was not talking about the European Pogroms. He was talking about demonstrations in places like Boston, which prides itself on being a city that embodies American liberalism, tolerance, and multiculturalism.

I grew up in Boston, and know from personal experience that this belief has always been marred by a measure of hypocrisy. And indeed, as has occurred so often in the past, none of these principles now appear to apply to the Jews. At one demonstration in Boston, several pro-Israel students were "surrounded by pro-Palestinian activists chanting 'Jesus killers' and 'drop dead'" before being physically attacked. Said one witness, "Some phones were knocked out of our hands, Israeli flags were yanked, and a whole lot of disgusting things were shouted at us." Another stated, "They said some nasty things, like calling us Jesus killers, asking how many babies we had each murdered, telling us we would burn."

And as in Europe, there appeared to be a disturbing indifference on the part of the authorities. Chloé Valdary, a prominent pro-Israel activist at the University of New Orleans, testified, "There were several cops who literally did nothing."

Perhaps the most disturbing thing, however, was the testimony of Californian activist Bea Lieberman:

> What I saw today was actually less ugly than we see in California. There were far fewer jihadi young men here covering their faces and holding flags of [Hezbollah leader Hassan] Nasrallah, chanting "slaughter the Jews." Where I'm from, there would be bars and police physically separating the protesters, because there are jihadi men who literally want to kill you.

If the standard of decency in Boston has now been lowered to simply being kind enough to refrain from outright genocidal rhetoric and intent to murder, then one wonders how much further one of America's most ostensibly liberal cities has to fall. Perhaps it will fall as far as Berlin, or Antwerp, or Paris.

Or perhaps it will fall as far as Calgary, where an entire family was assaulted by a mob of anti-Israel pogromists, sending several of them to the hospital.

"The victims," wrote the Washington Free Beacon,

> said they were just trying to express their support for Israel when an angry mob of pro-Palestinian demonstrators surrounded them, began shouting anti-Semitic slogans, and then proceeded to aggressively beat the family, which

included a 22-year-old girl and a 52-year-old woman who
had recently had stomach surgery.

The "antisemitic slogans" included "baby killers," "kill
Jews," and "Hitler should finish you off." Which are, of course,
not simply slogans, but also death threats. One of the victims
describes the pogromists attacking her 19-year-old brother. "He
had a Star of David on his shirt," she testified, "and they were
ripping it off, biting him, and scratching him, and stomping on him
on the ground."

Her mother, "who had recently gotten out of surgery for a
hernia, was spit on, 'punched in the stomach, and knocked down as
well.'"

> I was screaming and crying and some guy there decided he
> wanted to punch me in the face. I also got punched in the
> back of the head by a man. Then, somebody came up
> behind me and pulled my hair to pull me to the ground so
> they could run over and stomp on me.

It appears that, unsatisfied with beating up a woman, the
pogromists then attempted to murder her cousin: "They grabbed
me by my Israeli flag and pinned it around my neck and pulled me
to the ground and kept kicking me," he said. "Then they even drug
me down the street very briefly, dragging me by the neck by my
Israeli flag." He was ultimately chased through traffic by over two
dozen pogromists.

That a family of defenseless people had been attacked by a
group of thugs over ten times as large did not appear to bother the
Calgary police. Instead, they blamed the family for coming to the
demonstration with an Israeli flag. The local media did more or
less the same. That several of them could have been killed—as in
France, as in Berlin, as in Antwerp, as in Austria, as in any place a
pogrom occurs—did not matter either.

Indeed, another victim of the Pogrom, this time in
Montreal, drew a chilling parallel to the situation in France. The

victim, a French Orthodox Jew, was attacked in the street by what was described as "a young Arab man." The man who came to his aid said, "He kept saying 'this is Paris all over again. Quebec is going to be the new France.'"

Even in New York, a city of a million Jews, this "new France," the France of the Global Pogrom, is threatening. A branch of the Israel Discount Bank was attacked and vandalized by pogromists who "defaced the front windows and sidewalk with fake blood." One witness stated, "The employees were holed up inside and the doors were locked. No police presence beforehand."

Another employee described people "with flags basically screaming about the bank funding terrorists and some other nonsense."

> They made a scene with paint. It was like someone was shot—there was all red paint on the window which was washed afterwards. So obviously, it was not a safe environment as we were not allowed to go outside and afterwards we were told we better leave work by 3:30 because they are going to come back.

As far as can be ascertained, just as in Boston, Calgary, Montreal, and places like L.A. and Seattle where other incidents have been reported, no one has been arrested or charged in the incident.

And the Pogrom is still expanding. It has already spread as far as Australia, which has long called itself "the lucky country," due to its avoidance of most of the world's upheavals. Thanks to the Global Pogrom, this is no longer the case. Anti-Israel protests have sparked pogromist activity there as well. The Times of Israel reports that "a Melbourne man was attacked for wearing a shirt with the IDF logo and Hebrew writing" by two "Arabic speaking men" who shrieked "Jewish dog!" and "Allahu Akbar," as well as "something about Gaza in Arabic."

And shortly after the Gaza ground operation began, the blood libel found itself resurrected in the "lucky country." A billboard was unfurled showing a horrendous caricature of Israeli Prime Minister Benjamin Netanyahu adorned with fangs that dripped blood. He was bent over a child, and above were the words "can't get enough." The irony is palpable, as it appears to be the Global Pogrom that "can't get enough" of another people's blood.

Nowhere is the hatred, racism, and violence that drives the Global Pogrom more powerful than in the Muslim world. There, anti-Semitism appears in its most vulgar and debased form. It publicly embraces such demented myths as the blood libel and the Protocols of the Elders of Zion, which are usually only whispered in polite circles in the West. Though not, perhaps, for much longer, should the pogromists have their way.

Fortunately, but also tragically, however, the Muslim world has few targets for its hatred besides Israel. Its own Jewish communities, particularly in the Arab nations, were summarily ethnically cleansed following Israel's creation.

Only in one place in the Muslim world does a substantial Jewish community survive: Turkey. And it is they who have become the favored target of the Global Pogrom in the Muslim world itself.

They number only 17,300, but they are a strong and ancient community. In fact, the Jewish presence in Anatolia precedes Islam by at least 1,000 years, if not more. Yet the Global Pogrom has struck them too, particularly after the rise of the Islamist AKP party to power, and the resultant reawakening of publically expressed anti-Semitism.

Their awakening to the Global Pogrom came early, and it was notably brutal. In 2003, two synagogues in Istanbul—home to what is by far the largest Jewish community in the country—were hit by truck bombs. 27 people were killed.

The situation has only grown worse. And in recent weeks, it has reached a fever pitch, with the AKP and its Prime Minister Recep Tayyip Erdogan spewing antisemitic rhetoric against Israel and, by implication, his own Jewish community.

In one particularly vicious speech, Erdogan sounded the Nazi libel, saying that the Israeli offensive against Hamas "surpassed what Hitler did to them," meaning, of course, to all Jews. "Those who condemn Hitler day and night," he howled murderously, "have surpassed Hitler in barbarism." Israel, he said, was "spitting death, spitting blood," awakening again the blood libel that Jews drink the blood of gentiles.

In tandem, a newspaper described as "affiliated" with Erdogan and his party spat anti-Semitism at Turkey's Jewish community. One journalist penned an "open letter" to the country's chief rabbi. In one hideous passage, he shrieked, "You have lived comfortably among us for 500 years and gotten rich at our expense. Is this your gratitude—killing Muslims? Erdogan, demand that the community leader apologize!"

In addition, the chief of the IHH, a terrorist-associated NGO, openly threatened the Jewish community, saying "Turkish Jews will pay dearly" and "Tonight and tomorrow we are going to hold a different kind of protest, we do not have patience anymore."

And, of course, there was mob violence, this time directed against the Israeli consulate and the ambassador's residence. There was the usual stone-throwing, attempts at infiltration, and genocidal racism. One piece of graffiti left by the pogromists read "Die out murderer Jew!" and demanded Israelis "get out of Palestine," a frequent reference to the desire for the Jewish state's extermination.

There is another intended result of all this violence and murderous rhetoric: Turkish Jews are leaving. I know from talking with some of those who have made *aliyah* to Israel that the general attitude is a simple one: The younger generation no longer feels it has a future in Turkey. Within a generation, this ancient community will likely no longer exist.

In Turkey, in other words, the Global Pogrom has become an act of expulsion and ethnic cleansing.

And Turkey is not alone. The remains of another ancient community are also in the sights of the pogromists. *The Jerusalem Post* recently reported that in Morocco, regarded as one of the more tolerant nations in the Arab world, a rabbi was assaulted and beaten "over Gaza." Few Jews remain in North Africa, and soon—one imagines—the cleansing will be complete.

But to see the real implications of this slow ethnic cleansing, we must again look the epicenter of the Global Pogrom: To France. Seven decades after it handed most of its Jews over to extermination, it is now acquiescing to their expulsion.

As the *Los Angeles Times* recently reported,

> Last month, the Jewish Agency for Israel, which coordinates migration to Israel, said 1,407 of France's estimated 500,000 Jews left for Israel in the first three months of the year, four times more than for the same period in 2013.
>
> In 2013, 3,288 French Jews left for Israel, a 72% increase from the year before, and the first time French émigrés outnumbered those from the United States.

French Jews are quite open about their reasons for *aliyah*. One new *olah*, arriving in the midst of the Gaza war, told the Huffington Post that "I came because of anti-Semitism. You see it in the eyes of people. I see it in everything."

One of the world's most impressive men has weighed in on the implications of this act of ethnic cleansing. In an interview with the writer Liam Hoare published just a few days ago, in the wake of the French pogroms, legendary Russian dissident Natan Sharansky, current head of the Jewish Agency, pronounced a terrible judgment on a continent that appears to have both betrayed its Jews once again and forfeited its right to be called a civilization.

"I believe we are seeing the beginning of the end of Jewish history in Europe," Sharansky said.

> For more than 12 years, rabbis and teachers in French schools have told Jewish children not to go out in the street wearing a kippah. That's something that even Moscow and Kiev rabbis don't say to children. The fact that this started

in 2003 and 2004, during the Second Intifada, made people think it would be temporary. But it hasn't changed and it's not going to.

He described this as "an impossible situation for Jews," creating a "feeling of non-belonging and disengagement."

Sharansky also openly acknowledged—perhaps the first time a public figure has done so—what this really means: Expulsion and ethnic cleansing. Europe, in other words, has returned to the Middle Ages, when Jews were routinely expelled from one region to another.

He calls this a potential "exodus" of Europe's Jews as a whole. And he pointed out a terrible truth: "The leaders of Europe," he claimed, "have to think how they came to the point where Europe was once willing to give away millions of its citizens—its Jews—and now when the remnants of these Jews are willing to give away Europe."

And with terrible irony, he notes something else: That if and when this happens, "Europe will die here and survive in Israel."

There is a Global Pogrom under way. I say the terrible truth once again because it must be said again. It is a Pogrom undertaken by Muslims, Christians, atheists, and all those in between, all across the world. It is aided and abetted by the collaboration, indifference, and silence of the authorities—and of the world. It operates with impunity. It has murdered, it has maimed, it has destroyed lives and property, it has made life impossible for Jews in numerous countries, and it is now committing a crime against humanity: Expulsion and ethnic cleansing.

So the terrible truth must be spoken: Things must be called what they are—groups and individuals that commit violence against Jews, whatever they may call themselves, are not "activists," "protesters," or "demonstrators." They are pogromists. The movement that enables them is not pro-human rights, it is not anti-war, and it is not pro-Palestinian. It is a Global Pogrom. Groups that deny or engage in apologetics for their violence are hate groups.

So the terrible truth must be spoken: There is now, for all practical purposes, no distinction between hatred of Israel, hatred of Zionism, and hatred of the Jews. There may once have been a distinction. It is possible. But there is no longer, because the pogromists themselves have destroyed it.

So the terrible truth must be spoken: The Global Pogromists' motives are obvious—to intimidate Israel's supporters into silence; to partake in the inherent pleasure of violence and barbarism that exists in all of us; and the most simple and obvious motive of all, to brutalize, slaughter, and expel a people against whom they have ignited an inferno of racist hatred.

So the terrible truth must be spoken: If it is not stopped, the Global Pogrom will spread. It will spread to wherever there are large Muslim populations that embrace a culture of genocidal racist hatred. It will spread to wherever there are Leftists whose hatred of Israel has led them to the inevitable embrace of anti-Semitism. And it will spread to wherever the neo-Nazi and neo-fascist Right is once again ascending to power on a wave of discontent. And most of all, it will spread to wherever there are Jews to serve as targets.

So the terrible truth must be spoken: The Global Pogrom is an existential threat to the Jews. But not only the Jews. It is an existential threat to democracy, to civil society, and to civilization itself. Should Europe, the Muslim world, North America, and wherever else the Global Pogrom has spread wish to retain their status as civilizations, they must say no to the barbarism that is the Global Pogrom.

Because, as David Ben-Gurion once said, this is not a question of the Jews and the Arabs. It is a question of the Jews and the world. The world's responsibility to one of its smallest minorities is clear. And the fulfillment of such responsibilities is a mark of a true civilization. The question now is whether or not it will choose to forsake it entirely.

Yet amidst all of this horror, this return to a medieval barbarism we once hoped humanity had transcended; this realization that the world has still not, and perhaps never will learn its lesson; we are permitted to appreciate a transcendent irony.

Despite the prodigious horrors it has already committed, the Global Pogrom has also proved stunningly self-defeating. In its savage violence and hatred, it has served to confirm the Zionist case, create more *aliyah* to Israel, and drive the Jews of the Diaspora to once more take up arms in their own defense. It has, in other words, strengthened the country and the people it loathes with such a murderous passion.

But this small consolation is still a small one. And it is no substitute for justice. For the Global Pogrom to be defeated, justice must be demanded. Justice must be demanded for its victims and its targets. And justice must at long last be done upon its perpetrators.

So the final, most terrible truth must be spoken: This justice is the real test. If the world cannot or will not resist the Global Pogrom, then it cannot do justice. And if it cannot do justice, then it has forfeited its right to call itself a civilization. It has said yes to barbarism, and so has become barbaric itself. Because the essence of civilization, the one true justification for its existence, is to say no to barbarism. If the civilizations that have thus far said yes to the Global Pogrom will not decide, at long last, to say no; if they will not decide, at long last, to become civilizations again; then we must speak the terrible truth that Chaim Nahman Bialik spoke in the wake of a different but no less terrible pogrom: "Let the throne be hurled down forever."

The Global Pogrom, *Charlie Hebdo*, and the Future of Europe

On January 13, 2015, a major European politician finally said what every major European politician should have been saying for the past 15 years. In the wake of the January 7 slaughter of nearly the entire editorial staff of the satirical magazine *Charlie Hebdo*, followed by the January 9 hostage stand-off at the Hyper Cacher kosher supermarket that left four hostages dead—both committed by members of the same terror cell—French Prime Minister Manuel Valls rose to address the National Assembly on not only the threat of Islamic terror, but its connection to a hatred that, thus far, has dared not speak its name.

"History has taught us," he said, "that the awakening of anti-Semitism is the symptom of a crisis for democracy and of a crisis for the Republic." He then reiterated the butcher's bill of atrocities that have been committed against French Jews since the beginning of the second intifada in 2000, including the torture and murder of Ilan Halimi, the slaughter of a rabbi and several children at a Jewish school in Toulouse, and a series of brutal pogroms last summer in which rampaging mobs attacked a synagogue and trashed a Jewish neighborhood in Paris.

"Anti-Semitic acts in France have grown to an intolerable degree," Valls asserted, and admonished his fellow citizens for failing to express "the national outrage that our Jewish compatriots expected." With a sweeping overview of modern French-Jewish history, and breaking the unspoken taboo on discussing French collaboration in the Holocaust, he asked,

> How can we accept that in France, where the Jews were emancipated two centuries ago, but which was also where

they were martyred 70 years ago, how can we accept that cries of "death to the Jews" can be heard on the streets? How can we accept that French people can be murdered for being Jews? … This time it cannot be accepted … we must stand up and say what's really going on.

Valls speech broke another, even more potent taboo when he connected what he called "a new anti-Semitism" to "loathing of the State of Israel," a loathing that "advocates hatred of the Jews and all the Jews," echoing an earlier statement he made to Jeffrey Goldberg of *The Atlantic*, in which he spoke of a "radical criticism of the very existence of Israel, which is anti-Semitic. There is an incontestable link between anti-Zionism and anti-Semitism. Behind anti-Zionism is anti-Semitism." And Valls did not shrink from speaking the very uncomfortable truth that much of this anti-Semitism is coming from France's Muslim community, from "the difficult neighborhoods, from immigrants from the Middle East and North Africa, who have turned anger about Gaza into something very dangerous. Israel and Palestine are just a pretext. There is something far more profound taking place now."

But perhaps Valls' most pointed statement was also the simplest. "Without its Jews," he said, "France would not be France. … When the Jews of France are attacked, France is attacked, the conscience of humanity is attacked. Let us never forget it."

From another politician, such a statement might seem maudlin and empty. But Valls has put his money where his mouth is. This is not the first time he has denounced anti-Semitism in such terms; he has pursued hate speech prosecutions against prominent French anti-Semites; he has publicly stated that, since the Paris atrocities, "France is at war against terrorism, jihadism, radicalism"; and he was almost alone among French politicians in attending a local memorial service at the Hyper Cacher market.

But this speech may be his most important act yet. Because in it, he at last gave voice to a truth Europe has long silenced: The continent that gave us the Renaissance, the Enlightenment, and modernity itself now stands at a crossroads. It has a choice between the civilization it has painstakingly built, or a new barbarism of which anti-Semitism is an essential part. And it is by no means clear which choice Europe will make.

Prime Minister Valls' speech was potentially epoch-making. But he is only one man. Thus far, no other major French or European politician has made a statement of such purpose and ferocity.

Nonetheless, there are some signs that people are beginning to listen. At the massive January 11 rally in Paris, in which over a million people marched in solidarity with the *Charlie Hebdo* dead, for the principles of free expression, and against terrorism, the instantly famous slogan "Je suis Charlie" ("I am Charlie") appeared everywhere, but there were also signs saying "Je suis Juif" ("I am a Jew"). Throughout the procession, Israeli flags flew without fear for the first time in years. Despite objections, Israeli Prime Minister Benjamin Netanyahu not only attended, but managed to push himself to the front of the procession. From a building overhead, someone shouted "Am yisrael chai!" ("The people of Israel live!"). For a brief moment, after over a decade of alienation and apprehension, the Jews seemed to be at one with France again.

French-Jewish philosopher Bernard-Henri Levy, one of the French Left's staunchest defenders of Israel and Judaism, appears to believe that the march represents genuine change. "We have never seen anything like it before," he wrote. "Perhaps it was the straw that broke the camel's back and made a nation come out and say no to the barbarity for which for too long we have made too many excuses." Although there will be more Islamic terror, Levy wrote, "There will be fewer and fewer people who will whisper that we must keep a low profile and make accommodations." Equating radical Islam with the rise of far-Right parties in Europe, he stated, "From now on, all of Europe will no longer choose between the two versions of nihilism that are Islamism and populism." Ultimately, he believes, "One thing is for sure: France is no longer afraid."

There has also been the arrest of Dieudonne, an alleged comedian who is openly anti-Semitic, mocks the Holocaust, and developed the "quenelle," a variation on the Nazi salute that has become a popular fad. Shortly after the atrocities of January 9, he posted on Facebook, "Tonight, as far as I'm concerned, I feel like Charlie Coulibaly," expressing solidarity and identification with the Hyper Cacher murderer. The French, it seems, are finally getting serious about enforcing their hate speech laws against anti-Semites.

Some movement has also taken place on the international level. U.S. President Barack Obama, in his State of the Union address, spoke out against "the deplorable anti-Semitism that has resurfaced in certain parts of the world." Levy himself gave the keynote speech at a meeting on anti-Semitism at the notoriously anti-Israel United Nations, denouncing "the renewed advance of this radical inhumanity that is anti-Semitism." A UN spokesman stated, "Based on the available records we were able to check, this is indeed the first time that anti-Semitism as such is specifically the subject of an informal meeting of the UN General Assembly." The meeting was convened at the request of 37 member countries. That is, at least, a beginning.

The overall trends, however, are less encouraging. There is little doubt that "Je suis Charlie" vastly outnumbered "Je suis Juif" at the Paris rally; and one cannot imagine anything even close to such an outpouring of grief and outrage if the Hyper Cacher market had been the only target. French-Jewish concerns, to put it mildly, have yet to be assuaged. And French Jews are acting accordingly.

Perhaps the most pointed expression of this was made by Stephen Pollard, who edits *The Jewish Chronicle*, the United Kingdom's largest Jewish newspaper. "Every single French Jew I know," he told the *Daily Mail*, "has either left or is actively working out how to leave. ... It is the largest emigration of Jews anywhere since the war. That's a simple fact."

In the aftermath of the Hyper Cacher attack, it was easy enough to understand why. Thousands of French soldiers and police deployed across Paris to guard Jewish sites; Jewish neighborhoods went into lockdown, with businesses asked to close and most residents too frightened to leave their homes; and, most shamefully, the Grand Synagogue of Paris was closed for the first time since the end of the Nazi occupation in 1945.

Paris was not alone. An article in i24 News noted, "Heightened security measures, visible and non-visible, were swiftly enacted at Jewish places of worship, study and business across Europe over the weekend," including in Italy, Britain, Poland, the Netherlands, Germany, and Austria. Threats against the Swedish Jewish community doubled, prompting intervention not only by the police, but the intelligence services. For several days, Jewish life in Europe either ground to a halt or went on under what were, essentially, siege conditions.

The reaction of many in the media was also less than comforting. There have always been those ready to blame the Jews for anti-Semitism and anti-Semitic violence; and after the Paris attacks, they came crawling out of the woodwork with predictable speed. One BBC reporter seemed to personify French philosopher Alain Finkielkraut's recent observation that some feel the Jews are "responsible for what is happening to them, because of Israel's so-called racism and because Jews identify with Israel."

Speaking with the daughter of a Holocaust survivor at the Paris rally, Tim Willcox remarked, "Many critics ... of Israel's policy would suggest that the Palestinians suffered hugely at Jewish hands as well." When the woman pointed out the obvious fact that the Israeli-Palestinian conflict neither negates nor justifies atrocities committed against French Jews, the reporter responded, with nearly epic obtuseness, "But you understand, everything is seen from different perspectives?" The BBC later called the query "poorly phrased" and said that Willcox "had no intention of causing offense" by asking what any thinking person would regard as a stunningly offensive question.

Others simply demonstrated the indisputable fact that anti-Semitism is, at least on some level, a psychological disorder. Members of the Boycott, Divestment, and Sanctions movement, which advocates economic and diplomatic warfare against Israel and, for the most part, opposes its existence, exhibited particularly acute symptoms of the disease. One leader of the movement, Greta Berlin, used the telling "all caps" technique to announce "MOSSAD just hit the Paris offices of Charlie Hebdo in a clumsy false flag designed to damage the accord between Palestine and France. ... A four-year-old could see who is responsible for this terrible attack." The co-founder of Berlin's organization chimed in on Twitter, using a defamatory term comparing Israel to the barbaric terrorist group ISIS to say, "#Hebdo killings indefensible. Can't help thinking #JSIL Mossad false flag though."

Among some French Muslims, sentiments were equally disturbing, sometimes straying into the territory of the fantastic. In an article on what it called "jihad fanboys," The Daily Beast **noted** one young Muslim man saying the attacks were "a conspiracy designed by the Jews to make Muslims look bad." A schoolteacher was quoted saying "80 percent of his students didn't want to observe" the national moment of silence for those killed in the attacks, with one remarking, "You reap what you sow." The student promptly descended into pure science-fiction, asserting that the Paris attacks were

> "*un complot*," or conspiracy, and launched into a lengthy explanation of the "magical Jews" behind it. They were not ordinary Jews, he said, but a "hybrid race of shape shifters" who have extraordinary abilities. "They know how to get in everywhere," he said. "They are master manipulators."

And perhaps the surest sign that France has yet to fully understand the extent of the problem, and its own failure to deal with it effectively, is that anti-Semitic attacks have yet to cease.

The very day after the prime minister's speech, a Jewish library outside Lyon was vandalized by an assailant who shouted, "We will get the Jews!" A week later, a 13-year-old Jew wearing a *kippa* was attacked with mace by three teenagers euphemistically referred to as "of North African descent."

Compared to the Paris atrocities, of course, these are relatively minor incidents; but taken in context, they are no less disturbing. As France's National Bureau for Vigilance Against Anti-Semitism put it, they are part and parcel of a larger phenomenon in which "A child of 13, as he is about to celebrate bar mitzvah, knows nothing but the climate of fear and insecurity as a result of anti-Semitism."

In this context, it is not surprising that French Jews have little faith that their country will heed Valls' call to arms. The uncomfortable truth is that, while France was shocked by the Paris attacks, French Jews were not. And they blame it on a decade of indifference and inaction on the part of their countrymen.

Boaz Bismuth, writing from a Jewish neighborhood in Paris just after the attacks, noted,

> In my many visits to France, my Jewish acquaintances had told me that rising anti-Semitism would ultimately result in violence. It was just a matter of time, they warned. ... None of the Jews I met told me that they were surprised by what happened.

Roger Cukierman, the head of CRIF, France's largest Jewish organization, told him, "After French Jew Ilan Halimi was kidnapped and tortured to death in 2006, I said the Jews of France were all in danger. In 2012, when three children and one man were killed by a gunman at the Ozar Hatorah school in Toulouse, I doubled down on that statement." The attention and action that should have followed did not come. And, as one member of the community told Bismuth, "Just look at how much of an impact the jihadists have, and this is all because the French Republic let them."

French Jews' lack of faith in their country and countrymen seemed most emphatically demonstrated at the memorial service for the victims of the Hyper Cacher attack, held at the reopened Grand Synagogue. Both French President Francois Hollande and Israeli Prime Minister Benjamin Netanyahu attended, but it was Netanyahu alone who was given a hero's welcome, as the audience cheered and shouted, "Bibi, help us!"

In his speech, Netanyahu made sure to emphasize that *aliyah* was always an option for France's beleaguered Jews, and there is no doubt that more and more of them are availing themselves of it. Anyone who has lived in Israel for any length of time can see it. French has suddenly become commonplace on the streets of Tel Aviv, French cafes and bookstores are springing up everywhere, and in Netanya, a major center of French immigration, locals are beginning to grumble that the high number of new arrivals is driving up housing prices.

It does seem likely that *aliyah* will skyrocket in the wake of the attacks; indeed, the Jewish Agency has already reported as much. The reasons are simple enough. One of Bismuth's interviewees, whose son is already planning to make *aliyah*, simply said, "We have no reason to stay here"; while a prominent rabbi told his congregation after the attacks, "I know you want me to provide you with an answer on whether you should leave or stay. But frankly, I am at a loss for words."

But this *aliyah*, like so many others, will be a bitter exodus. One man asked Bismuth, "What have I done to deserve this constant worry about the lives of my kids to the point that I have to relocate?" Another said, "I am a big boy but on Friday I cried. I am already 60. Of course, I am planning to make *aliyah*, but I never thought I would ever leave France like this."

Perhaps the most devastating statement on the subject came from Norman Lebrecht in the *Telegraph*. A Jew whose family has lived in France for centuries, he echoed Valls' attack on his countrymen's indifference, saying that over a decade of anti-

Semitism "aroused no national outrage on the scale seen in the past week." As a result, "Jews fled in their thousands" and the march of millions through Paris in solidarity with the victims of Islamic terrorism has not convinced him that this will change. "My Jewish friends were out on the streets of Paris this weekend," he wrote, "hoping that, after this tragic moment, the tide will turn. For myself, I am unable to pretend that life will go on as before. My history, as a Jew of France, is over."

One must face precisely what this means: It is ethnic cleansing by any other name. Slowly but surely, the Jews are being expelled; if not by outright violence, then by depraved indifference. The Jews, in other words, are not abandoning France; France is abandoning the Jews.

A friend of mine said as much to me only a few days ago. On the night after the *Charlie Hebdo* attacks, a solidarity rally was held outside the French ambassador's residence in Tel Aviv. My friend, who made *aliyah* from France several years ago, refused to go. After Halimi was murdered, she said, they did nothing. After Toulouse, they did nothing. Now, because non-Jews have been killed, the nation is in mourning. To her, the hypocrisy was too much to take. France did not deserve her solidarity. Valls' speech was fine, she said, but talk is just talk. And she also does not believe things will change. "In ten years," she told me, "everyone will be gone."

My friend may prove to be right. It may be that, ultimately, Manuel Valls' *J'accuse* will fall upon deaf ears. Perhaps France does not particularly care what happens to its Jews. Perhaps it considers them a small sacrifice to make in order to appease Islamic terrorism and violence. But now that this violence has also struck not only at French gentiles, but at one of the most treasured principals of the French republic—the right to free expression— such indifference may, at long last, no longer be possible. Perhaps Valls will succeed in shattering the wall of denial France has built around itself and the rise of anti-Semitism.

One must hope this will be the case. Because in radical Islam, France, Europe, and indeed the world are now facing a new totalitarianism—an absolute threat to human rights and human freedom. Europe has faced this enemy before. In the past, communism, fascism, and Nazism have threatened liberal democracy in Europe. Now, Europe must understand that it faces a new, theocratic form of its old nemesis.

And it was no coincidence that Hannah Arendt began her epic work *The Origins of Totalitarianism* with a study of anti-Semitism. To a remarkable extent, Europe's battle for freedom has been a battle for the freedom of its Jews. And this is especially the case in France. From the decision by the French revolutionaries to emancipate the nation's Jews; to the battle to liberate Alfred Dreyfuss, which drew a stark line between the supporters of French democracy and its authoritarian opponents; to the bitter war between those who resisted and those who collaborated with Nazism—the struggle for liberal France has been, to one degree or another, a struggle against anti-Semitism.

Cukierman, who leads CRIF, said this explicitly after the Paris attacks. "Our democracy and our values are in the jihadists' crosshairs," he said, "and the Jews are on the frontline because they represent some of the values terrorists want to destroy." At the Grand Synagogue memorial service, Joel Mergui, who heads the Consistoire Israélite Central de France, **echoed** these sentiments, saying,

> Today France was in the streets, all of France … and the Jews of France were also in the streets to defend freedom of expression, to defend Charlie, to defend our democracy … because the Jewish people are democracy. … The hatred of Jews and the hatred of democracy are the same thing and must be fought in the same way.

If anything confirms Mergui's remarks, it is, ironically, the non-Jewish target of the Paris attacks. As Paul Berman wrote eloquently in Tablet, "*Charlie Hebdo* is a pure product of the

1968-era radical left—anti-authoritarian, insurgent, impudent, indignant, mocking, and self-mocking." Its founders, one of whom was murdered in the attack, "were fixtures of the '68-era alternative press in Paris," and friends of none other than Jean-Paul Sartre, the icon of modern French philosophy.

Charlie Hebdo, in other words, is another iteration in a long and venerated French tradition, stretching back as far as Rabelais, Voltaire, and de Sade—the tradition of satire, skepticism, free and even reckless speech, and the furious mockery of authority and power that is, in its own way, an essential expression of freedom. In attacking *Charlie Hebdo*, Islamic totalitarianism tried to drive a knife into the heart of France itself.

And the French should have seen it coming, because, as Valls himself put it, to attack the Jews is also to attack the heart of France. "To understand what the idea of the republic is about," he said,

> You have to understand the central role played by the emancipation of the Jews. It is a founding principle. If 100,000 French people of Spanish origin were to leave, I would never say that France is not France anymore. But if 100,000 Jews leave, France will no longer be France. The French Republic will be judged a failure.

But the French didn't see it coming, because they did not want to see it. For over a decade, they chose to believe that they were only coming for the Jews. It is now clear that this is not and never was the case. But unless France comes to understand this, and act accordingly, then Valls' dark prophecy will prove true: The French Jews will leave, and "France will no longer be France."

For France, and indeed all of Europe, this is a fateful moment. It can choose to act decisively against anti-Semitism, and in doing so secure justice for its Jews and a liberal and democratic future for themselves; a future in which its Jewish citizens do not live in fear of racist violence and its artists do not live in fear of being slaughtered by tyrannical fanatics. It can realize that to fight anti-Semitism is to fight Islamic terrorism itself. Or it can let its Jews flee, and find itself facing the specter of a new totalitarianism alone.

First they came for the Jews, the old adage goes, then they came for everybody else. It remains to be seen whether everybody else will understand this in time. They should hope that they do. Unlike the Jews, they have nowhere else to go.

Fighting the Global Pogrom

The worldwide eruption of anti-Semitism and anti-Semitic violence that is now over a decade old—and which I described as a Global Pogrom in a previous article—reached a peak during last summer's Gaza war and the subsequent series of terror attacks in Paris; but it shows no sign of dissipating. In Copenhagen, yet another attack on a group of artists who offended the delicate sensibilities of murderous fanatics was matched with yet another attack on a Jewish target—this time a synagogue in which a bat mitzvah was underway—leaving a volunteer security guard dead. It was later revealed that, unsurprisingly to those of us who have followed the phenomenon for any length of time, the Danish authorities had refused to provide enhanced security for the site.

Meanwhile, Jewish life across the Continent continued under a state of siege, with enhanced security thankfully provided in some countries, while Jewish leaders in others were left demanding more to little response. There was also Zvika Klein's now infamous video, in which he filmed himself walking the streets of Paris in a *kippah* and *tzitzit* to a seemingly endless torrent of intimidation and abuse, the perversity reaching a climax when a young child asked his mother, "Doesn't he know he'll be killed?" Even children, it seems, have become aware of the fact that, in many places in Europe, it has been decided that some have earned the right to attack and even kill Jews.

As was inevitable, moreover, the Pogrom has risen up against those who have denounced it. Most prominent among the targets was French Prime Minister Manuel Valls, who delivered a blistering denunciation of anti-Semitism after the Paris attacks, and has now been accused of being under the insidious control of his Jewish wife by none other than a former foreign minister of his own country.

Some pointed out the decision of a large group of Muslims to form a "peace ring" around a synagogue in Norway as a ray of hope. There is no doubt that it was an admirable example of interfaith solidarity. But if the Jews of Norway can now only worship under Muslim protection, serious questions must be raised about the ability or the willingness of the responsible authorities to take effective action.

Most disappointing of all, perhaps, was the most prominent example of Pogrom denial in years. In an interview with the website Vox, U.S. President Barack Obama made the no doubt well-meaning statement that the Paris kosher market attack was the act of "a bunch of violent, vicious zealots who … randomly shoot a bunch of folks in a deli in Paris." Given that the now-dead attacker openly acknowledged his anti-Semitic motivations, had cased other Jewish sites before the attack, and had asked at least one shopper if he was Jewish before shooting him after learning he was, the criticism that came the president's way cannot be viewed as anything other than fair. Even more depressing, however, was the fact that his statement was defended by several other administration officials, including the White House press secretary, who doubled down by saying the Jews at the Hyper Cacher market were targeted "because of where they randomly happened to be." The fact that Obama likely had the best of intentions when he made his statement makes it all the more disheartening, as it proves that Pogrom denial need not be malicious or even conscious in order to be extremely counterproductive.

In the face of all of this, it is easy enough to simply throw up one's hands in despair. The Global Pogrom, it seems, is unstoppable. No atrocity it commits will force the relevant authorities to acknowledge the threat, or convince those who could arrest its spread to act. There will be no justice for its victims, and no justice done upon its perpetrators. The Jews of Europe and wherever else the Pogrom has spread will flee, probably to Israel, and that will be the end of it.

But this is not the case. The Global Pogrom is not unstoppable. It is, in fact, extremely vulnerable. It has not been stopped because no one has seriously tried to stop it. It operates with impunity because it has been granted impunity, and that impunity can be taken away. If action is taken, and taken now, the Global Pogrom can be stopped, and it can be defeated.

There is no doubt that a Global Pogrom requires a global response. And, first and foremost, that must be a global Jewish response. But this has yet to be forthcoming. In particular, the U.S. and Israel, one with a large and politically active Jewish community, the other a militarily-empowered Jewish state, have proven disappointingly inactive on the issue. American Jewish organizations register protests, but have yet to undertake an organized campaign. Israel tends to urge *aliyah*, which, while admirable in and of itself, cannot solve the immediate problem. Put simply, Israel and the American Jewish community are the natural leaders of the struggle against a Global Pogrom, but they have yet to find a way to lead.

The reasons for this are fairly simple: For both American and Israeli Jews, the idea of a Global Pogrom is difficult to comprehend. American Jews have achieved unprecedented success and acceptance in the United States. It is all but inconceivable to them not only that a mass anti-Semitic movement might exist, but that the authorities would do next to nothing about it. To American Jews, anti-Semitism is not a mob of thugs attacking a synagogue or trashing a Jewish neighborhood, but a lone band of skinheads or members of a tiny Right-wing militia; and they have a justified confidence that the authorities will act to contain such domestic extremists.

As a result, a situation in which anti-Semitism is not simply the domain of kooks and rednecks, but a mass movement that has seized the imagination of millions across Europe, is very difficult for American Jews to grasp; let alone the possibility that authorities might act not with swift justice, but with indifference, idleness, denial, and even apologetics for the attackers.

In Israel, the problem is even simpler: Israeli Jews live in a country where they are a comfortable majority. They do not simply trust the state; they *are* the state. In effect, they live in a country in which the state *cannot* be anti-Semitic. As a result, for most Israelis—especially native-born *sabras*—the idea of a state that is simply unconcerned with anti-Semitism and its victims is so far beyond the realm of their personal experience as to be almost impossible to imagine. And, ironically, the possibility of *aliyah* has exacerbated the problem. After all, Israelis can say, if it's so bad over there, why don't they just come here?

In an irony even more tragic, these two communities are also hampered by the memory of the Holocaust. There is no doubt that, in comparison to the Shoah, the current wave of anti-Semitism pales in comparison. But since all such outbreaks are inevitably, if usually unconsciously, compared to the Holocaust, it is difficult for both American Jews and Israelis to see the Pogrom as serious enough to arouse apprehension and action.

And it is true: The Global Pogrom, thankfully, is not the Holocaust. Very, very far from it. But this does not make it in any way acceptable. Nor is it an excuse for allowing it to continue unchecked. The words "Never Again" do not only refer to the Holocaust, but to all forms of anti-Semitism and anti-Semitic violence, especially those that are officially condoned or officially denied. If that "Never Again" can be revived, however, in regard to the thankfully smaller but nonetheless horrifying phenomenon we currently face, then there is no doubt that Israel and American Jewry can rise to the occasion, as they did in the case of the Soviet Jews four decades ago. And as they were then, they can be victorious.

The most important thing for Israelis, American Jews, and indeed everyone to understand about the Global Pogrom is that the myth of its invincibility is just that. In fact, the Pogrom is strikingly vulnerable. Practically everything it does, from hate speech to physical violence to murder, is patently illegal. Many of these crimes also leave pogromists and their supporters open to civil penalties, such as the favorite pogromist tactic of destroying property. And, of course, the Pogrom violates the civil rights of citizens living in countries where civil rights are ostensibly sacrosanct. Indeed, to a striking extent, the Pogrom is most vulnerable to the weapon the relevant authorities are most frightened to use—namely, the enforcement of their own laws.

Even more important, perhaps, is the fact that—contrary to its portrayal in much of the media—pogroms are not the work of "random" individuals. Even the three perpetrators of the *Charlie Hebdo* and Hyper Cacher attacks were members of a carefully organized terror cell tangentially connected to al-Qaeda. But in the case of larger-scale attacks, some very prominent and very vulnerable groups are involved.

The mob that attacked and almost breached the gates of the Synagogue de la Roquette in Paris last summer, for example, did not emerge from a vacuum. It broke off from a much larger anti-Israel demonstration nearby. Such demonstrations do not happen spontaneously. They require money, organization, and equipment that only specific groups can provide. Without them, the Pogrom could not exist. In the case of the Paris pogrom, the demonstration was organized by a motley crew of Muslim and far-Left groups united around hatred of Israel. A similar situation took place in Britain. Demonstrations in Berlin that included genocidal rhetoric from various speakers also included attendees from far-Right and neo-Nazi organizations. Since even those demonstrations that did not descend into violence were marked by hate speech and incitement to violence, both of which are completely illegal in most European countries, all of the organizations involved in these incidents are exposed to civil and criminal penalties.

There is also the question of civil and religious leaders who engage in incitement to violence. Radical imams across Europe, for example, have been filmed and recorded giving sermons and speeches of the most vicious kind, quoting anti-Jewish sections of the Quran and demanding holy war against Israel and the Jews in general. Such sentiments are sometimes echoed by other public figures, few of whom face legal or civil consequences for their hate speech. But as the case of Dieudonné—an anti-Semitic French comedian just arrested for expressing solidarity with the Hyper Cacher terrorist—proves, the consistent enforcement of hate speech laws can be very effective.

In North America, where the Pogrom has struck in places like Boston, New York, and Calgary, the violence has been much less ferocious, but is clearly getting worse. There, the focal point is mostly college campuses. Perhaps because anti-Israel sentiment is widespread in institutions of higher education, perhaps because college administrations act, in a sense, as autonomous states-within-a-state, the European pattern is beginning to assert itself. Anti-Israel groups like Students for Justice in Palestine, for example, have openly used hate speech, incitement, and at times outright physical violence to intimidate Jewish and non-Jewish opponents. For the most part, the administrations in charge have reacted with little if any action, preferring—like the governments of Europe—to either pretend it isn't happening or blame it on the Jews themselves. Yet the conduct of groups like SJP is both patently illegal and in obvious violation of the speech codes that institutions of higher education enforce with great ferocity when other minority groups are involved.

Were these laws and other codes of conduct enforced consistently, were those who participate in mob violence against Jews arrested and criminally charged, were radical imams and anti-Semitic public figures consistently charged with racist incitement, were campus hate groups penalized or banned, and were groups that sponsor demonstrations at which hate speech and incitement lead to open violence held civilly and criminally liable for the damage they cause, the Global Pogrom would find itself seriously impeded and, ultimately, unable to function.

But it is now clear that none of this will happen without pressure. European governments, for the most part, either do not want or are too cowardly to enforce their own laws; and colleges and universities appear to feel the same way. It seems that the world will not act against the Pogrom unless it is forced to. And the only way to force it is to set the price of inaction higher than that of action.

And this pressure must come, first and foremost, from the global Jewish community; in particular, from American Jewry and Israel. To steal a line from Rabbi Hillel: If we are not for ourselves, who will be for us?

Contrary to the anti-Semitic stereotypes embraced by the global pogromists, the Jews do not rule the world, as the inability of the European Jews to garner more protection from their governments has amply demonstrated. But American Jewry and Israel have some cards they can play.

The model for such efforts is, as mentioned above, the struggle to free the Soviet Jews. With Israel acting as a destination for *aliyah* and a diplomatic player on the world stage, and American Jews engaging in a campaign of legal and political activism, as well as civil disobedience, the campaign on behalf of the Soviet Jews was ultimately successful. There is no reason to think that the same kind of campaign cannot be successful in arresting and defeating the Global Pogrom.

The first and most important aspect of this is awareness. Israel and American Jewry must learn to think beyond the safety of their own societies and understand the sense of vulnerability and powerlessness felt by their brothers and sisters in Europe and elsewhere. The second is to use this awareness to foster solidarity and organization. The Jewish community is not yet global, but it can become so. To my knowledge, there are, as yet, no organizations, ad hoc or otherwise, dedicated solely to fighting the Global Pogrom. The existence of one, hopefully with representatives from all Jewish communities around the world, and funded mainly by American Jews and the Israeli government, is an essential first step.

Moreover, we have other models that demonstrate the success of specific tactics. The recent multi-million dollar judgment against the Palestinian Authority for engagement in terrorism is an excellent example. Organizations like Shurat HaDin, which pursued the case against the PA, and the Southern

Poverty Law Center, which has successfully litigated against American white supremacist groups, have shown that victims of racist violence can financially damage the individuals and organizations behind this violence, and sometimes drive them into bankruptcy and outright collapse.

Political advocacy can be equally effective. There is no doubt that the European Jews lack an advocate, and a global anti-Pogrom organization backed by Israel and American Jewry can fill this vacuum. Indeed, properly undertaken, it could immensely aid in such causes as disabusing the U.S. administration of its unfortunate misconceptions in regard to the Pogrom, puncturing Europe's sense of moral superiority on the subject, and pressuring governments and institutions to consistently enforce the laws and regulations that would cripple the Pogrom's ability to commit violence and incitement.

In the media and cultural realm, advocacy against the Pogrom and its accomplices should concentrate on urging the press to give more coverage to the problem, and to expose and ostracize pogromists, as well as their defenders and apologists. Advocacy can also go a long way toward seizing the moral high ground and shifting perceptions, demanding that things be called what they are: This wave of anti-Semitism is not a series of isolated incidents; authorities are not doing enough to stop it; the Arab-Israeli conflict is neither relevant to nor an excuse for those who engage in racist violence; campus organizations that use intimidation and incitement against their opponents are hate groups; anti-Israel demonstrations that devolve into anti-Jewish hate speech and violence are not demonstrations but pogroms; the phenomenon of mass emigration is not an exodus but an expulsion; and the world is morally culpable for its inaction.

In addition, an effort must be made to understand that the struggle against the Pogrom is not just a Jewish struggle. Although it is sometimes hard to find them, the Jews do have allies, such as the aforementioned Manuel Valls. It is necessary, even imperative, to include them as part of any anti-Pogrom organization. The Jews have some power, but if only by sheer numbers, non-Jews have much more. The Jews often have few friends, and should never turn away from those willing to make a stand against anti-Semitism and the Global Pogrom to which it has given birth.

All of this may seem a daunting task, and it is; but there is no doubt that it is a battle that can be won. And it can be won because, besides savagery, the most prominent quality of the Pogrom is cowardice. It only attacks soft targets, and usually when the pogromists' overwhelming numbers grant them a sense of safety and impunity. The Global Pogrom is the work of cowards, and cowards can be deterred.

But none of this will happen unless action is taken, and it must first be taken by the global Jewish community and its allies. And it must be taken now. Because one thing has become eminently clear: We can't wait.

Why can't we wait?

First, there is the simple fact that the Pogrom has already claimed too many victims. It has steadily escalated from individual acts of violence, such as the murder of Ilan Halimi and the Toulouse massacre, to full-scale mob attacks against Jews and Jewish sites. And like most diseases, if left untreated, it will get worse. As journalist Ben Cohen has noted, the Pogrom has already become a mass movement, and if it is not stopped, it could well result in mayhem and murder on a much larger scale. Again, it is not the Holocaust; but the casualty rate is already unacceptable, and there is no reason to think it will not rise precipitously if action is not taken.

Second, the Jews of Europe and countries such as Turkey are facing what can only be described as a *de facto* expulsion. Life for them is becoming impossible, and they are acting accordingly. *Aliyah* rates are already skyrocketing; and many European Jews are seriously considering other options, such as the UK or the United States. This is, of course, an understandable response, and one to which the Jews have unfortunately adapted over the course of centuries. But we should not turn away from what it is: Whether by indifference or design, the expulsion of a people is a crime against humanity. And all people have a moral obligation to prevent such things by whatever means necessary to do so. And if these means are not employed, and employed soon, the wave of emigration may well become impossible to arrest. Five centuries after the expulsion from Spain and 70 years after the Holocaust, the world will, in effect, have consented to another, if less terrible, crime against humanity and the Jewish people.

Third, there is no question that, should it continue to operate unchecked, the Pogrom will spread. Indeed, it has already done so. During the Gaza War, as noted above, attacks were reported in the U.S., Canada, Australia, Turkey, and other countries well beyond the borders of Europe. As also noted, college campuses in North America are quickly becoming incubators of the disease. The American and other non-European Jewish communities likely feel that their distance from the epicenter of the Pogrom will keep them safe, but this is very unlikely to be the case. Mass movements, anti-Semitic or otherwise, almost always become larger if they are not effectively checked; and large Jewish communities, including in the United States, will be far too tempting a target should the Pogrom reach critical mass outside Europe.

Fourth, there is the consequence that thus far has dared not speak its name: In the face of official inaction, there are those in the European Jewish community who have decided that the Jews must be protected by any means necessary, and they are swiftly gaining popularity and power as a result. With anti-Jewish violence reaching unprecedented levels, and lacking any trust in the authorities, Jews are turning to their own extremists, including groups whose politics are dangerously radical.

The most prominent of these groups is the LDJ, a French offshoot of the Jewish Defense League. Embracing the extremist ideology of the late Meir Kahane, they are perfectly willing to use violence in the defense of the Jewish community; and as the situation worsens, they have risen in membership and esteem. Having participated in the successful defense of the la Roquette synagogue, they are now regarded as heroes by some in the French Jewish community, and the failure of the authorities to effectively protect the synagogue has leant some credibility to this claim. If more effective action is not forthcoming, we may well find more and more young Jews embracing the LDJ as their only shield against anti-Semitic violence. As one older member of the French-Jewish community said after last summer's pogrom, "The LDJ is our Iron Dome."

This should be a sobering thought for many. It takes a great deal to push the Jews to violence, but when it happens, we are often very good at it. In a terribly ironic twist, the French authorities may soon face a situation in which their Jews have become so radicalized that they will undertake not only exodus, but an armed struggle. And the first Diaspora revolt in 2,000 years, spearheaded by a Kahanist group, would be neither good for Europe nor good for the Jews.

Finally, there is the simplest but most important question: The question of justice. The nations of Europe and the international community in general have for decades based their laws and their rhetoric on the idea that persecution on the basis of race or religion constitutes not only a legal but a moral injustice. Thus far, however, they have turned away from justice in regard to the global Jewish community. The victims and targets of the Global Pogrom deserve justice, a justice too long deferred. The struggle against the Pogrom is, in short, a moral struggle, a struggle for universal justice, and the world has an obligation to act accordingly. But if the struggle does not begin now, the situation may well reach the point at which justice is impossible.

"In every generation," reads the Haggadah, "they rise up to destroy us." No amount of denial can change an indisputable fact: They have risen up again. And they must be stopped.

We can't wait. Neither can the world. It is time for this generation's struggle for justice to begin.

9 781511 744522